Black Mountain Poems

Black Mountain Poems

AN ANTHOLOGY

edited, with an introduction,
by Jonathan C. Creasy

A NEW DIRECTIONS
PAPERBOOK ORIGINAL

Cover photo: Harriet Sohmers Zwerling, *The Studies Building and Lake Eden, Black Mountain College, 1949*. Courtesy of the Black Mountain College Museum + Arts Center

Manufactured in the United States of America

First published as a New Directions Paperbook Original (NDP1464) in 2019

Library of Congress Cataloging-in-Publication
Names: Creasy, Jonathan C., editor, writer of introduction.
Title: Black Mountain poems / edited, with an introduction, by Jonathan Creasy.
Description: New York, N.Y. : New Directions Publishing Corporation, 2019.
Identifiers: LCCN 2019020097 | ISBN 9780811228978 (alk. paper)
Subjects: LCSH: American poetry—20th century. | Arts, American—20th century. | Black Mountain College (Black Mountain, N.C.)
Classification: LCC PS583 .B53 2019 | DDC 811/.5208—dc23
LC record available at https://lccn.loc.gov/2019020097

10 9 8 7 6 5 4

New Directions Books are published for James Laughlin
by New Directions Publishing Corporation
80 Eighth Avenue, NY 10011

Contents

Grouping writers into "schools" has always been problematic. The so-called Black Mountain Poets never identified themselves as such, but the facts of their union spring from a remarkable instance of artistic community—Black Mountain College and the web of interactions the place occasioned. Founded in the mountains of western North Carolina in 1933 and closed by 1956, the college was one of the most significant experiments in arts and education of the twentieth century. In recent years, a number of international exhibitions and publications have appeared showcasing the range of artwork produced at the college's two campuses, the first situated in the YMCA Blue Ridge Assembly, and the second at Lake Eden in the Swannanoa Valley. The list of famous names associated with Black Mountain is as impressive as it is unlikely, given that the college never housed more than a hundred students and faculty at a time, often far fewer.

Difficult questions persist in attempting to define a "Black Mountain" school of poets. Do we look to the physical and historical circumstances of Black Mountain College, or the complex pattern of friendships, influence, correspondence, publication, and collaboration that constitute the broader notion of this artistic coterie?

Charles Olson, the nucleus of what we have generally considered Black Mountain poetry, began teaching at the college in 1948 and became its final rector in 1953. In 1954, he brought Robert Creeley—Olson's "Figure of Outward"—to Black Mountain. By that time there were fewer than twenty students in residence. However, through a network of relationships and correspondence emanating from Olson's "little hot-box of education," the instigations of Black Mountain College made an impact on artistic circles in New York, San Francisco, Los Angeles, and elsewhere. The "open field" poetics of Olson, Creeley, and Robert Duncan in particular have influenced generations of poets. Still, the supposed Black Mountain school of poetry is difficult, if not impossible, to define. Olson said himself,

I think that whole "Black Mountain Poet" thing is a lot of bull-shit. I mean, actually, it was created by the editor, the famous editor of that anthology, Mr. Allen.... There are people, for example, poets, who just can't get us straight, because they think we form some sort of a what? A claque or a gang or something. And that there was a poetics? Boy, there was no poetics. It was Charlie Parker. Literally, it was Charlie Parker.

Donald Allen's anthology, *The New American Poetry 1945-1960*, in-cludes poets Olson, Duncan, Creeley, Denise Levertov, Paul Black-burn, Paul Carroll, Larry Eigner, Edward Dorn, Jonathan Williams, and Joel Oppenheimer under the Black Mountain banner. Allen makes this selection based on publication in two important little magazines of the 1950s, *Origin* (edited by Cid Corman) and the *Black Mountain Review* (edited by Creeley from 1954 to 1957). Two small presses, Creeley's Divers Press in Mallorca and Williams's Jargon Press, founded in 1951 just before he arrived at Black Mountain, published early works by many of these writers.

Critics and editors have also argued that the Black Mountain Poets can be understood in relation to Olson's "projective verse" essay from 1950, in which he argues for a breath-metered poetry that breaks free from "that verse which print bred." Yet, just as he rejected the idea of Black Mountain poetry, Olson diminished the importance of his 1950 essay. Much of his work is concerned with the visual elements of poetry on the page as well as with sound pro-jected on the breath. Susan Howe, one of Olson's poetic inheritors, argues that the "feeling for seeing in a poem, is Olson's innovation," and that this vision separates Olson's epic, *The Maximus Poems*, from his predecessors Ezra Pound and William Carlos Williams and their verse epics, *The Cantos* and *Paterson*. Poems can be performative, but also plastic and pictorial.

In reference to Black Mountain, Olson once told Creeley, "I need a college to think with." The intense artistic community shaped Olson's work and marked him as a distinctly pedagogical poet. Creeley once remarked that his voluminous correspondence with Olson leading up to their first meeting at Black Mountain was "of such energy and calculation that it constituted a practical 'college' of stimulus and information." The profound creative and personal relationship between Olson and Creeley, both teachers at the college, is one window into the poetry and poetics associated with Black Mountain. Yet the story goes much deeper. As Olson says, it was "Charlie Parker"; it was improvised, open-ended, subject to chance and change.

What is all too obvious is that Allen's grouping of Black Mountain Poets leaves out a number of writers who have more to do with Black Mountain than some of those who appear in *The New American Poetry*. Olson, Creeley, and Duncan taught at Black Mountain, and Dorn, Oppenheimer, and Jonathan Williams were students there. Levertov and Blackburn never set foot in Black Mountain, while students like John Wieners and poet-teachers like Mary Caroline Richards and Hilda Morley are left out of Allen's book and many other important anthologies of U.S. poetry. Olson rejected the idea of a common Black Mountain poetics, but if we look to the actual facts of the college—the teaching, learning, and experimentation that went on there, and the extraordinary artists on its grounds and in its orbit—we find certain elements of process, form, and content that reveal shared aims in their work.

The college's founder John Andrew Rice envisioned an institution that would take the "progressive" model as professed by John Dewey and push it further toward a new vision of education within democracy. It was not an art school. Rather, in line with Dewey's thinking, the college's goal was to provide a well-rounded curriculum that placed the arts at its center. Rice is quoted in a 1936 article on Black Mountain, published in *Harper's Monthly*,

> Here our central and consistent effort is to teach method, not content, to emphasize process, not results; to invite the student to the realization that the way of handling facts and him amid the facts is more important than the facts themselves....
>
> There is a technic [sic] to be learned, a grammar of the art of living and working in the world. Logic, as severe as it can be, must be learned; if for no other reason, to know its limitations.

> Dialectic must be learned: and no feelings spared, for you can't
> be nice when truth is at stake.... Man's responses to ideas and
> things in the past must be learned. We must realize that the world
> as it is isn't worth saving; it must be made over. These are the
> pencil, the brush, the chisel.

Though the founding principles laid out by Rice in the 1930s rarely come into discussion of the Black Mountain Poets, I can think of no better statement to unify the group of writers later associated with the college. Another founder, Theodore "Ted" Dreier, writes, "Black Mountain has stood for a non-political radicalism in higher education which, like all true radicalism, sought to find modern means for getting back to fundamentals."

Black Mountain was not, however, isolated from the political realities of its time. We can point to the role the college played in the civil rights movement. In 1944, ten years before Brown v. Board of Education, the college took controversial steps to integrate the campus. The dissenters in the college did not object to racial integration. Rather, they were fearful of threats and reprisals from some of their neighbors in Buncombe County, North Carolina. One teacher wrote, "It is the better part of wisdom not to invite trouble by declaring open warfare against the South."

As an initial measure, the college decided to accept an African-American student, Alma Stone Williams, to the 1944 summer music institute. She became the first black student to integrate a white college in the South. In a memoir found in the Western Regional branch of the State Archives of North Carolina, Williams writes,

> Black Mountain could manage to integrate persons of diverse
> races, classes, nationalities, and physical conditions in its com-
> munity, but in Georgia, the state in which I was born, I was seen
> as one dimensional—Black.... The year was 1944. Though it
> wasn't easy for it to do so, Black Mountain College was ready
> for me; the rest of the white South, not yet.

While her situation was unique, Williams met other students and teachers at Black Mountain familiar with terror. From the beginning, the college's progressive experiment was shaped by a group of European émigrés fleeing authoritarian regimes in Europe. Principal among these figures were Josef Albers, the German painter and former Master in the Bauhaus, and his wife Anni Albers, the weaver and teacher. Anni was Josef's student in the Bauhaus, and they came to America together after the Nazis forced closure of the German art school.

Beginning in 1933, over sixteen years Josef and Anni were central to life at Black Mountain. Josef Albers's modified Bauhaus curriculum became the high standard for teaching at the college. His goal as a teacher, he said, was "to open eyes." This was the focus of education at Black Mountain: finding new perspectives, new ways of seeing and thinking about the world. These means were aesthetic, pedagogical, and—yes—political.

Albers's teaching later influenced poets at Black Mountain. As Duncan says of his own classes at the college,

> I just had what would be anybody's idea of what Albers must have been doing. You knew that [Albers's students] had color theory, and that they did a workshop sort of approach, and that they didn't aim at a finished painting ... I thought "Well, that's absolutely right" ... I think we had five weeks of vowels ... and syllables ... Numbers enter into poetry as they do in all time things, measurements. But ... [with] Albers ... it's not only the color, but it's the interrelationships of space and numbers.

Interactions and relationships were part of the shared artistic concerns at Black Mountain, but they were also simple facts of life in the community. Beside the Black Mountain Poets, one thinks of the incredible list of artists who spent time living, teaching, and studying at the college: Willem de Kooning, Elaine de Kooning, Franz Kline, Ruth Asawa, Cy Twombly, Dorothea Rockburne, Elizabeth Jennerjahn, Pete Jennerjahn, Robert Rauschenberg,

Kenneth Noland, Ray Johnson, Arthur Penn, Hazel Larsen Archer, Jacob Lawrence, Gwendolyn Knight, Merce Cunningham, Katherine Litz, John Cage, David Tudor, Lou Harrison, Stefan Wolpe, and the list goes on.

On the grounds of Black Mountain College, relationships between these artists created new works. For instance, Creeley collaborated with painter Dan Rice on the book, *All That Is Lovely In Men*, which includes some of Creeley's finest early work. Creeley and Rice lived together at the college and shared a deep love of jazz, an interest that shaped the rhythms and stuttering syntax characteristic of Creeley's lyric poems.

Olson participated in a "glyph exchange" with artist Ben Shahn and dancer-choreographer Katherine Litz, and he even attended some of Merce Cunningham's dance classes. William Carlos Williams, Albert Einstein, and John Dewey were all included in a list of the college's advisors. This gives a sense of how vibrant the artistic, intellectual, and social interactions at Black Mountain really were. It inspired focused attention and groundbreaking work, while—like any small, tightly knit community—it bred resentments and schisms that ultimately led to its end.

Many of the well-known figures at Black Mountain wrote poems, and when we look at the life of the college from 1933 to 1956, we see a much wider view of what might be considered Black Mountain poetry. This anthology highlights the breadth of poetry written in the context of Black Mountain College. While accepting the common Black Mountain Poets—Olson, Creeley, Duncan, Levertov, Dorn, Oppenheimer, Williams—it also points to writers not usually considered in this group. Albers is the heart of Black Mountain pedagogy, and he served as a link between the Bauhaus and Black Mountain, extending their influence in U.S. higher education through his later connections to Harvard and Yale. Like most of his artworks, Albers's poems are simple, direct, and economical.

John Cage taught at the college for short periods in the spring and summer of 1948 and summers of '52 and '53, and he made a profound impact on the community alongside his collaborator Merce Cunningham. Cage's *Theater Piece No. 1* (known as the first "happening") is one of the most famous events in Black Mountain's history and mythology. The improvised event included Olson and Richards reading poems, with contributions from Cunningham, Rauschenberg, and Tudor, among others. Cage's largely chance-derived writing, much of which he wrote to be performed as lecture-poetry, expands the space-time experiments of his musical compositions. Both Cage and Cunningham had valuable interactions with Buckminster Fuller at Black Mountain. During one summer session, Fuller erected the first geodesic dome of his design on the lawn at Lake Eden. I include sections of his *Untitled Epic Poem on the History of Industrialization* in this selection, as it is a unique articulation of Fuller's worldview and a curious instance of the ranging focus in both content and form we find in these poems.

Paul Goodman also taught briefly at Black Mountain, and I include him here as much for the significance of his political and pedagogical writings as his poetry. A fine poet, he authored seminal prose works of the era, including *Growing Up Absurd*, *Communitas*, and *Gestalt Therapy*. Goodman's work gives us a view into the profound shifts in society taking place in the United States in the 1940s and '50s. Black Mountain played a part in this shifting cultural landscape, and its instigations—like Goodman's writing—paved the way for counter-culture movements of the 1960s.

Both M. C. Richards and Hilda Morley have been neglected for far too long. Richards was one of the most beloved teachers at Black Mountain. In 1948, she founded the Black Mountain Press and she published the first edition of the *Black Mountain Review* (though it is possible that Olson and Creeley knew nothing of this earlier venture when they published their magazine in 1954). Black Mountain student Fielding Dawson writes, "We must rid our minds of the famous names that have come to identify the school. A fresh approach to comprehend and define Black Mountain, would be to place M. C. at narrative center, and define Black Mountain through her. She as much as anyone, far more than most, assumed its identity, absorbed it, no matter where she was." Dawson places Richards in direct contrast to Olson as a potential center of Black Mountain poetry, art, and education. After leaving Black Mountain in 1954, Richards joined Cage, Cunningham, and Tudor in Paul Williams's Stony Point community in Rockland County, New York. Olson later referred to Stony Point as a "continuing limb" of Black Mountain College.

Morley taught poetry at BMC, with a special interest in the Metaphysical poets. In 1952, she married Stefan Wolpe, the German composer who taught music at Black Mountain, and whom Olson refers to in the opening lines of "The Death of Europe." Wolpe suffered from Parkinson's disease for almost a decade before his death in 1972, and Morley wrote a beautiful book of elegies for him, *What Are Winds & What Are Waters*. Morley's work shows a deep and abiding interest in contemporary painters, as we see in her poem "The Eye Opened." In "For Creeley," she gives an indelible portrait of the young poet upon his arrival at Black Mountain. Creeley himself contrasts Morley's work with "the characteristic male proscriptions one had thought to learn and attend." He continues in a forward to her selected poems, *The Turning*, "I wonder at the way you taught yourself then to move with such lightness and particularity, touching each term and thing, each feeling, always making them actual— like Denise saying (quoting Jung), 'Everything that acts is actual.' You made remarkable sense of it."

In making the selections for this volume, I rely on years of keeping these poets close to my own heart and mind. The discovery of their work, and the attendant fascination with the people and place of Black Mountain College, has shaped my writing and thinking. Olson reminds us that "life is involvement with itself." The power of these poems exists in a ceaseless inward searching and outward projection of simple human truths through the activity of poetry— poems as the measure of a life. They are involved in scriptural communion and conversation.

★

Three key texts on the history of Black Mountain College ought to be consulted by interested readers: Martin Duberman's *Black Mountain College: An Exploration In Community*, Mary Emma Harris's *The Arts at Black Mountain College*, and *Black Mountain College: Experiment in Art*, an exhibition companion edited by the poet and scholar Vincent Katz. The more recent exhibition book, *Leap Before You Look*, edited by Helen Molesworth, is a beautiful addition to the literature. Many other critical studies have been written on Black Mountain artists and writers, along with biographies of the major figures. More of these books appear every year.

Both former campuses of the college are still standing and can be visited. The Western Regional Archives and the Black Mountain College Museum + Arts Center in Asheville, North Carolina, are key institutions and resources for the history and legacy of the college. I am grateful to both for their support.

This slim volume can only introduce the reader to a fraction of what these poets produced, and there are arguments to be made for the inclusion, or exclusion, of certain poets based on all kinds of criteria. This book cannot serve to represent all those who wrote poetry at Black Mountain College, nor can it fully account for the outsized influence Black Mountain Poets continue to have over the poetry landscape. What I hope is that readers will find something that rings true and follow up with the countless books and other works produced by each of these unique artists. A small selection such as this has its obvious limitations, but it also has certain virtues. I have traveled the globe with small books of poetry tucked into my pockets, constant companions in the search for new ways of seeing and feeling the world. My hope is that, for some, this volume becomes such a faithful friend.

JONATHAN C. CREASY
DUBLIN, IRELAND, 2019

Josef Albers

from *POEMS & DRAWINGS*

Life—the love of eternity
eternity—the love of life

★★★

My earth
serves also others

my world
is mine alone

★★★

IT WAS NOT MEANT TO BE

When thinking of you
it enters my head

why now are the blueberries red
and the black ones all eaten

and the only ripened apple

just run over by a car

when I want to walk it starts to rain

or someone comes to see me

besides all this the paint gave out

before the picture was finished

what now shall I aspire to

for so I was not meant to be

MORE OR LESS

Easy—to know

that diamonds—are precious

good—to learn

that rubies—have depth

but more—to see

that pebbles—are miraculous

★★★

There is no world without a stage
and no one lives for not-appearing

Seeing of ears invites to speak
knowing of eyes invites to show

Notice also, silence sounds
listen to the voice of color

Semblance proves it can be truth
as every form has sense and meaning

***

To distribute material possessions
is to divide them

to distribute spiritual possessions
is to multiply them

***

Calm down
what happens

happens mostly
without you

"The difficult problems are the fundamental problems; simplicity stands at the end, not at the beginning of a work. If education can lead us to elementary seeing, away from too much and too complex information, to the quietness of vision, and discipline of forming, it again may prepare us for the task ahead, working for today and tomorrow."

Anni Albers, *Black Mountain College Bulletin* (1941)

Anni Albers in her weaving studio at Black Mountain College (1937).

Photo by Helen M. Post Modley.
Courtesy of Western Regional Archives, State Archives of North Carolina

Charles Olson

THESE DAYS

whatever you have to say, leave
the roots on, let them
dangle

And the dirt

       Just to make clear
       where they came from

THE K

Take, then, my answer:
there is a tide in a man
moves him to his moon and,
though it drop him back
he works through ebb to mount
the run again and swell
to be tumescent I

The affairs of men remain my chief concern

We have come full circle.
I shall not see the year 2000
unless I stem straight from my father's mother,
break the fatal male small span.
If that is what the tarot pack proposed
I shall hang out some second story window
and sing, as she, one unheard liturgy

Assume I shall not.
Is it of such concern when what shall be
already is within the moonward sea?

Full circle: an end to romans, hippocrats and christians.
There! is a tide in the affairs of men to discern

Shallows and miseries shadows from the cross,
ecco men and dull copernican sun.
Our attention is simpler
The salts and minerals of the earth return
The night has a love for throwing its shadows around a man
a bridge, a horse, the gun, a grave.

THE DEATH OF EUROPE

(a funeral poem for Rainer M. Gerhardt)

Rainer,
the man who was about to celebrate his 52nd birthday
the day I learned of your death at 28, said:
"I lie out on Dionysius' tongue"!

the sort of language you talked, and I did,
correctly—
                as I heard this other German wrongly,
from his accent, and because I was thinking of you,
talking of how much you gave us all hearing
in Germany (as I watch a salamander on the end of a dead pine
        branch
snagging flies), what I heard this man almost twice your age say was,
"I lie out on a dinosaur's tongue"!

for my sense, still, is that,

despite your sophistication
and your immense labors ...

It will take some telling. It has to do with what WCW
(of all that you published in *fragmente*, to see Bill's
R R BUMS in futura!

                              it has to do with how far back are

Americans
as well as,
Germans

                    "walk on spongey feet
                    if you would cross

                    carry purslane
                    if you get into her bed

                    guard the changes
                    when you scratch your ear

|
It is this business
that you should die!
Who shot up,
out of the ruins,
and hung there,
in the sky,
the first of Europe
I could have words with:

as Holderlin on Patmos you
trying to hold bay leaves
on a cinder block!

Now I can only console you,
sing of willows,
and dead branches,
worry the meanness
that you do not live,
wear the ashes
of loss

      Neither of us
carrying a stick
any more

Creeley told me
how you lived

II
I have urged anyone
back (as Williams asked
that Sam Houston
be recognized
         as I said,
Rainer, plant
your ash

    "I drive a stake into the ground, isn't it silly,"
I said out loud in the night, "to drive a stake into the ground?"

How primitive

does one have to get? Or,

as you and I were both open
to the charge: how large

can a quote

get, he

said, eyeing me

with a blue

eye

                        Were your eyes

                        brown, Rainer?

                        Rainer,

                        who is in the ground,

                        what did you look like?

                        Did you die of your head bursting

                        like a land-mine?

                        Did you walk

                        on your own unplanted self?

III
It is not hell you came into,
or came out of. It is not moly
any of us are given. It is merely
that we are possessed of
the irascible. We are blind
not from the darkness
but by creation we are

moles. We are let out
sightless, and thus miss
what we are given, what woman
is, what your two sons
looking out of a picture at me,
sitting on some small hillside—

they have brown eyes, surely.

> Rainer, the thyrsus
> is down
>
> I can no longer
> put anything
> into your hands
>
> It does no good
> for me to wish
> to arm you
>
> I can only carry laurel,
> and some red flowers,
> mere memorials, not cut
> with my own knife an oar
> for you, last poet
> of a civilization
>
> You are nowhere
> but in the ground

IV
What breaks my heart
is that your grandfather
did not do better, that our grandmothers
(I think we agreed)

did not tell us
the proper tales

so that we are as raw
as our inventions, have not the teeth
to bite off Grandfather's
paws

(O, Rainer,
you should have ridden your bike
across the Atlantic instead of your mind,
that bothered itself too much
with how we were hanging on
to the horse's tail, fared, fared
we who had Sam Houston, not
Ulysses

                    I can only cry: Those
                    who gave you not enough
                    caused you to settle for
                    too little

                              The ground
                    is now the sky

V
But even Bill
is not protected,
no swift messenger
puts pussley
even in his hand,
open,

as it is, no one says how
to eat

at the hairy table
           (as your scalp
also lifted,
        as your ears
did not say

silk

               O my collapsed brother,
               the body
               does bring us
               down
                    The images
               have to be
               contradicted
                        The metamorphoses
               are to be
               undone

               The stick,
               and the ear

               are to be no more than

               they are: the cedar

               and the lebanon

               of this impossible

               life.

               I give you no visit

               to your mother.

What you have left us

is what you did

It is enough

It is what we

praise

I take back

the stick.

I open my hand

to throw dirt

into your grave

I praise you

who watched the riding

on the horse's back

It was your glory to know

that we must mount

O that the Earth

had to be given to you

this way!

O Rainer, rest

in the false

peace

Let us who live

try

MAXIMUS, TO HIMSELF

I have had to learn the simplest thing
last. Which made for difficulties.
Even at sea I was slow, to get the hand out, or to cross
a wet deck.
              The sea was not, finally, my trade.
But even my trade, at it, I stood estranged
from that which was most familiar. Was delayed,
and not content with the man's argument
that such postponment
is now the nature of
obedience,

              that we are all late
              in a slow time,
              that we grow up many
              And the single
              is not easily
              known

It could be, though the sharpness (the *achiote*)
I note in others,

makes more sense
than my own distances. The agilities

        they show daily
        who do the world's
        businesses
        And who do nature's
        as I have no sense
        I have done either

I have made dialogues,
have discussed ancient texts,
have throne what light I could, offered
what pleasures
doceat allows

        But the known?
This, I have had to be given,
a life, love, and from one man
the world.

        Tokens.
        But sitting here
        I look out as a wind
        and water man, testing
        And missing
        some proof

I know the quarters
of the weather, where it comes from,
where it goes. But the stem of me,
this I took from their welcome,
or their rejection, of me

And my arrogance
was neither diminished
nor increased,
by the communication

2

It is undone business
I speak of, this morning,
with the sea
stretching out
from my feet

KNOWING ALL WAYS, INCLUDING THE TRANSPOSITION OF CONTINENTS

I have seen enough: ugliness
in the streets,
and in the flesh I love

I have gone as far as I will go: justice
is not distributable, outside
or in

I have had all I intend
of cause or man: the unselected
(my own) is enough
to be bothered with. Today
I serve beauty of selection alone
—and without enormous reference to stones
or to the tramp of worms
in the veins. Image
can be exact to fact, or
how is this art twin to what is,

what was,
what goes on?

America, Europe, Asia,
I have no further use for you: your clamor
divides me from love,
and from new noises.

Robert Creeley

THE WHIP

I spent a night turning in bed,
my love was a feather, a flat

sleeping thing. She was
very white

and quiet, and above us on
the roof, there was another woman I

also loved, had
addressed myself to in

a fit she
returned. That

encompasses it. But now I was
lonely, I yelled,

but what is that? Ugh,
she said, beside me, she put

her hand on
my back, for which act

I think to say this
wrongly.

TWO WAYS OF LOOKING IN A MIRROR

At midnight the world is a mediate
perspective.
                      And hence
to an immaculate
bed, the time of

passion,
flowers of my mind. Consumptive
prayers keep us: the moon in its low chamber.

And about us, rayed out in a floral wall-
paper-like pattern, the

facts of our union. Bliss
is actual, as hard as
stone.

THE PICNIC
                for Ed and Helene

Ducks in the pond,
ice cream & beer,
all remind me
of West Acton, Mass—

where I lived when young
in a large old house
with 14 rooms
and woods out back.

Last night I talked
to a friend & his wife
about loons & wildcats
and how to live on so much money per month.

Time we all went home,
or back,
to where it all was,
where it all was.

THE RHYME

There is the sign of
the flower—
to borrow the theme

But what or where to recover
what is not love
too simply.

I saw her
and behind her there were
flowers, and behind them
nothing.

FOR W.C.W.

The pleasure of wit sustains
a vague aroma

The fox-glove (unseen) the
wild flower

To the hands come
many things. In time of trouble

a wild exultation

SOME PLACE

I resolved it, I
found in my life a
center and secured it.

It is the house,
trees beyond, a term
of view encasing it.

The weather
reaches only as some
wind, a little

deadened sigh. And
if the life weren't?
when was something to

happen, had I secured
that—had I, *had*
I, insistent.

There is nothing I am,
nothing not. A place
between, I am. I am

more than thought, less
than thought. A house
with winds, but a distance

—something loose in the wind,
feeling weather as that life,
walks toward the lights he left.

THE RAIN

All night the sound had
come back again,
and again falls
this quiet, persistent rain.

What am I to myself
that must be remembered,
insisted upon
so often? It is

that never the ease,
even the hardness,
of rain falling
will have for me

something other than this,
something not so insistent—
am I to be locked in this
final uneasiness.

Love, if you love me,
lie next to me.
Be for me, like the rain,
the getting out

of tiredness, the fatuousness, the semi-
lust of intentional indifference.
Be wet
with a decent happiness.

PAUL

I'll never forgive myself for the
violence propelled me at sad Paul
Blackburn, pushed in turn by both
our hopeless wives who were spitting
venom at one another in the heaven
we'd got ourselves to, Mallorca, mid-fifties,
where one could live for peanuts while
writing great works and looking at the
constant blue sea, etc. Why did I fight such
surrogate battles of existence with such
a specific friend as he was for sure?
Our first meeting in NYC 1950 we talked two
and a half days straight without leaving the
apartment. He knew Auden and Yeats
by heart and had begun on Pound's lead
translating the Provençal poets, and was
studying with Moses Hadas at NYU. How
sweet this thoughtful beleaguered vulnerable
person whose childhood was full of New
England abusive confusion, his mother the too
often absent poet, Frances Frost! I wish
he were here now, we could go on talking,
I'd have company of my own age in this
drab burned out trashed dump we call the
phenomenal world where he once walked
the wondrous earth and knew its pleasures.

"TO THINK ..."

To think oneself again
into a tiny hole of self
and pull the covers round
and close the mouth—

shut down the eyes and hands,
keep still the feet,
and think of nothing if one can
not think of it—

a space in whose embrace
such substance is,
a place of emptiness
the heart's regret.

World's mind is after all
an afterthought
of what was there before
and is there still.

"I got hold of copies of *The Black Mountain Review* and witnessed real excellence not only of content but design. One, a thick white-covered book, had a Dan Rice pre-minimalist abstraction that I thought was the hippest thing I'd ever seen."

Amiri Baraka, *The Autobiography of LeRoi Jones*

The Black Mountain Review # 6, cover by Dan Rice

Robert Duncan

OFTEN I AM PERMITTED TO RETURN TO A MEADOW

as if it were a scene made-up by the mind,
that is not mine, but is a made place,

that is mine, it is so near to the heart,
an eternal pasture folded in all thought
so that there is a hall therein

that is a made place, created by light
wherefrom the shadows that are forms fall

Wherefrom fall all architectures I am
I say are likenesses of the First Beloved
whose flowers are flames lit to the Lady.

She it is Queen Under The Hill
whose hosts are a disturbance of words within words
that is a field folded.

It is only a dream of the grass blowing
east against the source of the sun
in an hour before the sun's going down

whose secret we see in a children's game
of ring a round of roses told.

Often I am permitted to return to a meadow
as if it were a given property of the mind
that certain bounds hold against chaos,

that is a place of first permission,
everlasting omen of what is.

COME, LET ME FREE MYSELF

Come, let me free myself from all that I love.
Let me free what I love from me, let it go free.
For I would obey without bound,
serve only as I serve.

Come, let me be free of this master I set over me
so that I must exact rectitude
        upon rectitude,
right over right. Today

I am on the road, by the road,
hitch-hiking. And how, from one side,
how glad I am no one has come along.
For I am at a station. I am at home
in the sun. Not waiting, but standing here.

And, on the other, I am waiting,
to be on the way, that it be *my* way.
I am impatient.

O let me be free now of *my* way, for all that I bind to me
—and I bind what I love to me,
     comforting chains and surroundings—
let these loved things go and let me go with them.
For I stand in the way, my destination stands in the way!

THE STRUCTURE OF RIME I

    I ask the unyielding Sentence that shows Itself forth in the
language as I make it,

    Speak!   For I name myself your master, who come to serve.
    Writing is first a search in obedience.

There is a woman who resembles the sentence. She has a place in
memory that moves language. Her voice comes across the waters
from a shore I don't know to a shore I know, and is translated into
words belonging to the poem:

    Have heart,   the text reads,
      you that were heartless.
    Suffering joy or despair
    you will suffer the sentence
    a law of words moving
    seeking their right period.

I saw a snake-like beauty in the living changes of syntax.

    Wake up, she cried.
    Jacob wrestled with Sleep—you who fall into Nothingness
      and dread sleep.
    He wrestled with Sleep like a man reading a strong sentence.

I will not take the actual world for granted, I said.

Why not? she replied.
Do I not withhold the song of birds from you?
Do I not withhold the penetrations of red from you?
Do I not withhold the weight of mountains from you?
Do I not withhold the hearts of men from you?

I alone long for your demand.
I alone measure your desire.

O Lasting Sentence,
sentence after sentence I make in your image. In the feet that measure the dance of my pages I hear cosmic intoxications of the man I will be.

Cheat at this game? she cries.
The world is what you are.
   Stand then
so I can see you, a fierce destroyer of images.

Will you drive me to madness
   only there to know me?
vomitting images into the place of the Law!

THE STRUCTURE OF RIME II

What of the Structure of Rime? I said.

The Messenger in guise of a Lion roard: *Why does man retract his song from the impoverished air? He brings his young to the opening of the field. Does he so fear beautiful compulsion?*

I in the guise of a Lion roard out great vowels and heard their amazing patterns.

A lion without disguise said: He that sang to charm the beasts was false of tongue. There is a melody within this surfeit of speech that is most man.

What of the Structure of Rime? I asked.

An Absolute scale of resemblance and disresemblance establishes measures that are music in the actual world.

The Lion in the Zodiac replied:

The actual stars moving are music in the real world. This is the meaning of the music of the spheres.

THANK YOU FOR LOVE
(for Robert Creeley)

                        A friend
's a distant nearness,
as if it were *my* loneliness you have
given song to, given a hand

towards parting without faltering,
lingering in the touch.

Is serious grace your part
in this
tenderness regret enhances?

At the dance we were sad.
Turning aside to talk,
we did not talk but said

what we could say under stars
as they were. Confiding
is a pure gesture, of itself
dear. Towards meeting.

We only referrd to meeting,
a confidence
stumbling has towards moving on.
The feet are there

with us. Given the fact,

we will be moving on.
The song will be moving.
Words are friends
and from their distance

will return.

ANSWERING

(after CLARITAS by Denise Levertov)

A burst
of confidence. Confiding

a treasured thing

kept inside,
as if it were a burden,

worrying about money,
or were pride
and ambition struggling—

sing out.

It was a song I did not sing.

    ★

The men are working in the street.
The sound

of pick and pneumatic drill

punctuates
the chirrup a bird makes,

a natural will
who works the tossing dandelion head

—a sheaf of poems.

They are employd
at making up a joyous

possibility.

They are making a living
where I take my life.

    ★

With no more earnest skill
than this working song

sings
—as if the heart's full

responsibility
were in the rise of words

as momentarily
that bird's notes he concentrates

above the swaying bough,
the fluttering wings.

        ★

For joy
breaks thru

insensible to our human want.
Were we birds too

upon some blowing crown of seeds,
it would be so

—we'd sing as we do.

The song's a work of the natural will.
The song's a work of the natural will.

BRING IT UP FROM THE DARK

Bring up from the dark water.
It will be news from behind the horizon.
Refugees, nameless people.   Who are they?
What is happening?   I do not know.
Out there.   Where we can see nothing.
Where we can do nothing.   Men of our own country
send deadly messengers we would not send.
The cold wind of their desolation chills the first hint of morning,
of the dead men daily they kill rise
against us.   It will go against us,
    pass, sweep on and beyond us.

The great house of our humanity
no longer stands.   Men from our own country
stamp out, burn back, flush up from their refuge
with gasses, howling or silent, whatever
human or animal remains living there.

Bereft, the mothering sky
searches our faces, searches my heart.
What have I to do with these things
that now I am left destitute.
In the midst of my happiness, the worm
of man's misery coils in my heart.

Dream disclosed to me, I too am Ishmael.

Denise Levertov

ACTION

I can lay down that history
I can lay down my glasses
I can lay down the imaginary lists
of what to forget and what must be
done. I can shake the sun
out of my eyes and lay everything down
on the hot sand, and cross
the whispering threshold and walk
right into the clear sea, and float there,
my long hair floating, and fishes
vanishing all around me. Deep water.
Little by little one comes to know
the limits and depths of power.

WITH EYES AT THE BACK OF OUR HEADS

With eyes at the back of our heads
we see a mountain
not obstructed with woods but laced
here and there with feathery groves.

The doors before us in a façade
that perhaps has no house in back of it
are too narrow, and one is set high
with no doorsill. The architect sees

the imperfect proposition and
turns eagerly to the knitter.
Set it to rights!
The knitter begins to knit.

For we want
to enter the house, if there is a house,
to pass through the doors at least
into whatever lies beyond them,

we want to enter the arms
of the knitted garment. As one
is re-formed, so the other,
in proportion.

When the doors widen
when the sleeves admit us
the way to the mountain will clear,
the mountain we see with

eyes at the back of our heads, mountain
green, mountain
cut of limestone, echoing
with hidden rivers, mountain
of short grass and subtle shadows.

A COMMON GROUND

i
To stand on common ground
here and there gritty with pebbles
yet elsewhere 'fine and mellow—
uncommon fine for ploughing'

there to labor
planting the vegetable words
diversely in their order
that they come to virtue!

To reach those shining pebbles,
that soil where uncommon men
have labored in their virtue
and left a store

of seeds for planting!
To crunch on words
grown in grit or fine
crumbling earth, sweet

to eat and sweet
to be given, to be eaten
in common, by laborer
and hungry wanderer…

ii
In time of blossoming,
of red
buds, of red
margins upon
white petals among the
new green, of coppery
leaf-buds still weakly
folded, fuzzed
with silver hairs—

when on the grass verges
or elephant-hide rocks, the lunch hour
expands, the girls
laugh at the sun, men

in business suits awkwardly
recline, the petals
float and fall into
crumpled wax-paper, cartons
of hot coffee—

to speak as the sun's
deep tone of May gold speaks
or the spring chill in the rock's shadow,
a piercing minor scale running across the flesh
aslant—or petals
that dream their way
(speaking by being white
by being
curved, green-centered, falling
already while their tree
is half-red with buds) into

human lives! Poems stirred
into paper coffee-cups, eaten
with petals on rye in the
sun—the cold shadows in back,
and the traffic grinding the
borders of spring—entering
human lives forever,
unobserved, a spring element...

iii

> ... everything in the world must
> excel itself to be itself.
>
> *Pasternak*

Not 'common speech'
a dead level
but the uncommon speech of paradise,

tongue in which oracles
speak to beggars and pilgrims:

not illusion but what Whitman called
'the path
between reality and the soul,'
a language
excelling itself to be itself,

speech akin to the light
with which at day's end and day's
renewal, mountains
sing to each other across the cold valleys.

CLARITAS

i
The All-Day Bird, the artist,
whitethroated sparrow,
striving
in hope and
good faith to make his notes
ever more precise, closer
to what he knows.

ii
There is the proposition
and the development.
The way
one grows from the other.
The All-Day Bird
ponders.

iii
May the first note
be round enough
and those that follow
fine, fine as
sweetgrass,
          prays
the All-Day Bird.

iv
Fine
as the tail of a lizard,
as a leaf of
chives—
the *shadow of a difference*
falling between
note and note,
a *hair's breadth*
defining them.

v
The dew is on the vineleaves.
My tree
is lit with the
break of day.

vi
Sun
light.
     Light
light light light.

Buckminster Fuller's geodesic dome at BMC (summer 1949)

Photo by Masato Nakagawa.
Courtesy of the Western Regional Archives, State Archives of North Carolina.

R. Buckminster Fuller

from *UNTITLED EPIC POEM ON THE HISTORY OF INDUSTRIALIZATION*

PART II
During the first half of its history
the characteristic achievement
of the embryonic
United States of Northern America
was political.

It was the GREAT EXPERIMENT
in freedom of thought and expression
which drew three million pioneers to it
for a new way of life,
and new opportunity; —
despite ulterior motives
of land patent schemes.

Nothing did the successive
exploiters baggings
of bright eyed families
of colonists know
of the complete massacres
that had befallen
their falsely billed
"ground breaking" predecessors
at Head Tide
Pemaquid, Popham, Castine,
Wiscasset, Fox Island, Monhegan, and Bath
in Bay of Maine Royal Company grants!

So frightful to home subjects
and financially devestating
to shipbuilding investments
and empire exploitation
would news of these massacres
have proven to be, —
if reported back home, —
that fourteen long years
of such human under-plowing
were officially shushed
so that 1620, — instead of 1606, —
the king's original granting year, —
is popularly known as
the Pilgrim's premier.

But quite serenely —
as the sun draws a billion
tons of water each day
unseen into the sky
there to appear
as beautiful clouds
which in turn raining down
maintain life on earth —
by similar indirect cultivation
a great quality came to America.

Because pioneering
cannot abide
action through fear
the **achievement**
vacuum drafted
automatically and unnoticed
a pure
longing-dominated

basic genetic ingredient
from out the mixed
fear and longing
motivation-conglomerate
of the older world
into America.

In prosaic economics however
the achievement unfolded
as the net result
of **agricultural and craft ingenuity**
under highly cooperative measures
essential to hard
pioneering survival.

Not only building each other houses,
tilling each other's fields,
these free individuals also
gave their lives freely
for others.
Would fight their way
through thousands of miles of wilderness
to save one another.

Thus on the American frontier,
these three million pioneers from Europe
miraculously multiplied their numbers
not just through mating
but by the conservation of brotherhood
to a twenty-three million living population
between the years 1600–1850
despite a high rate of mortality.

During the second half of U.S.A. history,
that is, from about 1850 to present,
and especially during the twentieth century,
its characteristic achievement
has been INDUSTRIALIZATION.

During this period thirty-five million people
ferried across the Atlantic
in the new steamships
to the U.S.A.'s citied shores
for survival betterment.
This second phase is indeed
the logical outgrowth of the first.
It represents the fulfillment,
or the partial fulfillment,
of the opportunity that men came to seek.

Towards that opportunity
for a period of 340 years
three hundred and seventy million native born
offspring of from one to ten generations
of the original
thirty-eight million total migrants
to the United States portion of Northern America
have each in some measure
made contribution: —
grand totalling, numerically,
four hundred and eight million individuals
of whom one third are even now
much alive.

But genetically
the blood of the U.S.A.
is three parts to one
of the original pre-revolutionary
freedom loving and fearless
virulent pioneer fluid,
and nine to one native born
despite visible enormity
of immigrant slums,
a fact which world politicos
fail to grasp
though often stunned by its backfire.

PART XI
And that "it" isn't
is what your poet-painter has been trying to say
by vainly writing of what love **is**
what hate **is**
and what a rose, —
or any continuing process group
identified with **life**, —
is.

Paradoxically the poet's preoccupation
with describing the indescribable
and his disdainful neglect of the physical
for what it precisely is worth
allows him to fall
into the phsychological nature-trap
tended by those who exploit
such illusory preoccupations
with pragmatic glee.

That is they exploit him by dealing in fish
which only the poets can catch
with their creative imagination nets.

The pragmatists have only
to stand by with their baskets
infra-visible
to the ultra ranging spectrum of the poets,
as the latter throw the caught fish aside,
shimmering, flapping, and vital,
disdaining for the moment of even thinking
of consuming such beauty, —
and only intent on casting again.

But between fishing trips
our poet must buy
those fish again from the merchants,
smoked, grilled, or hashed.

Thus are the poets kept poor,
poor in eats, while rich in potential.

Poor poet eating with one hand
while writing his book with the other
is constantly positing
disproval of the love **abstraction**
which he weaves
by identifying life only
with the corporeal mechanism of ordination.

And what the poet wrote
which may live down the ages
was much more of his living soul
than was the hand of the body
which moved the pen.

Anyway it is very interesting, —
and artist, if you must be favored
in your insistance
that her legs **are Sylvia**
and the hand is man,
then also you must agree
that his eye glasses must also be man.

And also his chair
devised but two thousand years ago
as an extension of the monarchial fanny
by Mediterraneans for mobility purposes
while their Eastern cousins
still sat on the ground.

The eyeglasses and chair are
neither fungus, nor flower, nor rock outcropping.
They are phenomena that exist in the world
only because
man was there first.

Therefore it follows
that whether we hold with the artist's
or with the scientist's concepts
it is inconsequential
to the resultant under consideration
for either way
the **mechanical extension**
is still an articulated part of "man"
whether the extension be
of organic or inorganic substances
or only an ephemerally vibrated air word
electrically transcribed;
or "canned" for tomorrow.

NO MORE SECONDHAND GOD

The revolution has come —
set on fire from the top.
Let it burn swiftly.
Neither the branches, trunk, nor roots will be endangered;
only last year's leaves and
the parasite bearded moss and orchids
will not be there
when the next Spring brings fresh growth
and free standing flowers.
Here is God's purpose —
for God, to me it seems,
is a verb —
not a noun,
proper or improper;
is **articulation**,
not the art, objective or subjective;
is **loving**,
not the abstraction "Love" comanded or entreated;
is **knowledge dynamic**,
not legislative code,
not proclamation law,
not academic dogma, nor ecclesiastic canon.
Yes, God is a verb,
the most active,
connoting the vast harmonic
reordering of the universe
from unleashed chaos of energy.

"I want to congratulate you upon the work you are doing. You are here as a little community to work with your hands and your brains, which is a good thing for you. What is done out of pleasure is much better done than what is done out of duty. If you had to climb mountains out of duty, you could not mount these high mountains. I think that is also true with the high mountains of the spirit."

Albert Einstein on Black Mountain College

Paul Goodman

from *NORTH COUNTRY*

Our house in the hollow is hemmed in
        also by immense maple trees
but walk a short ways to the meadows
        or up the hills and sky and skies
shatter the world, it cannot hold
        against the gales of openness
whose clouds appear from nowhere
        and drift away southwest.
By the road a small daisy
        stands up among the horizons
a still wheel of eighteen spokes
        and a yellow hub that spins.

LONG LINES

At 20,000 feet the earth below was overcast
the flat top of the cloud was like a desert dusted with snow.
At my sunny porthole I agreed to be resigned
as in a bright hospital where they would feed me well
but like one peacefully dying rather than convalescent.
The sky was royal blue to the skim-milk horizon
and the sun was awash in its own golden light,
I stared at hungry with my weeping eyes.
Then were my cares for my sick country quieted
though not forgotten, and the loneliness
in which I ever live was quieted.
Briefly I dimly saw below the wide meandering,

among the Blue Ridge Mountains, Shenandoah River,
and one friendly sparkle from a wave
like a signal to me leaped across four miles of space
saying "God! God!" or "Man! Man!" or "Death!"
or whatever it was, very pleasantly.

from *LITTLE PRAYERS*

Sometimes I said I was marooned
sometimes that I was imprisoned
    or was in exile from my land
    or I was born on the wrong planet.

But my daily fact, Lord,
is that awake I am a coward
    and in my dreams that say the cause
    I have lost the address, I'm confused.

"Anarchism is grounded in a rather definite proposition: that valuable behavior occurs only by the free and direct response of individuals or voluntary groups to the conditions presented by the historical environment. It claims that in most human affairs, whether political, economic, military, religious, moral, pedagogic, or cultural, more harm than good results from coercion, top-down direction, central authority, bureaucracy, jails, conscription, States, preordained standardization, excessive planning, etc. Anarchists want to increase intrinsic functioning and diminish extrinsic power."

Paul Goodman, "Reflections on the Anarchist Principle"

M. C. Richards

THEY ARE SLEEPING

I have painted the female hills
stretched and piled against the sky.
They are sleeping.
I have given them golden haloes.
They are saints.
They are sleeping.
I have painted the gold in clouds and crevices as well,
meaning to say how they too are saints,
how the world sleeps,
how womanly is the landscape,
how a whiskered angel also sleeps, as a field of grain.

STRAWBERRY

In November
the strawberry hangs on a thread of sleep.
In May
it lies in my hand like an erotic dream.

HOMAGE TO THE WEINRIBS, POTTERS: BLACK MOUNTAIN COLLEGE

Sun-up /
over the valley's lip a running glaze,
lake, crazed and curdled.

Sun-down / and
the dense rim fires
nut-black, bone-brown.

Stoneware is the night,
its granite foot, aside, the hills,
trimmed sills and shallows. O bene,
bene,
blessed be the jars that
burn with day, turn smack
center on the whirring dark.

FOR KAREN KARNES, ON HER 37th BIRTHDAY

clay
has a way, of making seed streets for vagrant birds,
soup saddles to hold us thirsty riders,
clay corned to a bitter red
and straddled and thinned down to blue,
I say, clay
has a way of being plastic
and without residue, we sing
to the one who works it so.
We sing: soul, and shaper.

    This is a birthday
    This is Karen, devoted to the plainspeaking of clay
and its parables.
    This is our pleasure,
        To listen to her vessels' cuneiform,
        To respond with a verse
        and to love the speaking dust.

"CONCERTS OF SPACE"

For Lucy Rie

I was looking at a friend's bookshelf
                        this morning
and I thought I saw a book with the title:
                        "CONCERTS OF SPACE"
and my heart leapt!: "What a poetic title!" I exclaimed,
        (hearing music of the spheres and heavenly harmonies!)
And then my gaze lengthened, and the words read:
        "CONCEPTS" OF SPACE. Never mind, I said to myself,
                                (and perhaps aloud),
I shall write a poem and call it "Concerts of Space,"
and it shall be for Lucy Rie
        and the cup and saucer she made, and gave to me on Sunday.

Your pots are decisions, Lucy Rie,
        decisions, forms, and emblems: *mots*.
No, no, they are pots of clay,
timbres of darkness and light,
suffered through, come safely through.
Your hands, Lucy Rie, conduct them through the fire:
                        "concerts of space."

FOR JOHN CAGE ON HIS 75th BIRTHDAY

Dear John Cage
It is already dusk
and the cows are not yet in—
already dawn, are not yet out. Listen.
It sounds ever thus, the breathing.
40 years ago
you touched down at our landing,

young planets.
inwardly orbiting.   tirra lire loo
Our first words were a courtship!
tirra lira   day in and day out
Shall I tell you the secret of our mystery?
You are a preacher and I am a missionary.
We make love for justice
and delight: kindliness, laughter, and rage.
Macrobiotic eros, you nourish the ends of the earth
in ever new beginnings.
The cows, John, the cows are banging their udders
like soft cymbals, and the milkers
are playing the teats like bell ropes
tugging and letting go.
The music, my God, the music!

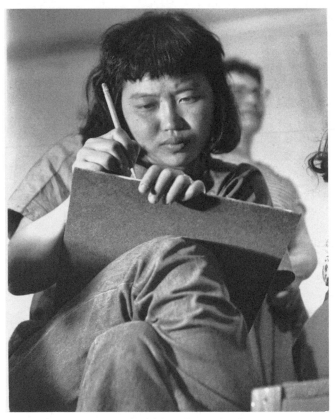

Ruth Asawa, Black Mountain College student from 1946–1949.

Courtesy of Western Regional Archives.

John Cage

from *SILENCE*

M.C. Richards and David Tudor invited several friends to dinner. I was there and it was a pleasure. After dinner we were sitting around talking. David Tudor began doing some paper work in a corner, perhaps something to do with music, though I'm not sure. After a while there was a pause in the conversation, and someone said to David Tudor, "Why don't you join the party?" He said, "I haven't left it. This is how I keep you entertained."

***

One day down at Black Mountain College, David Tudor was eating his lunch. A student came over to his table and began asking him questions. David Tudor went on eating his lunch. The student kept on asking questions. Finally David Tudor looked at him and said, "If you don't know, why do you ask?"

***

Music means nothing as a thing.
A finished work is exactly that, requires resurrection.

from *COMPOSITION IN RETROSPECT*

> you can't be serIous she said
> we were driNking
> a recorD
> was bEing played
> noT
> in thE place
> wheRe we were

but in another rooM
I had
fouNd it interesting
And had asked
what musiC it was
not to supplY

a partIcular photograph
but to thiNk
of materials that woulD
makE
iT
possiblE
foR
soMeone else
to make hIs
owN
A
Camera
it was necessarY

for davId tudor
somethiNg
a puzzle that he woulD
solvE
Taking
as a bEginning
what was impossible to measuRe
and then returning what he could to Mystery
It was
while teachiNg
A
Class
at wesleYan

that I thought
of Number II
i haD
  bEen explaining
variaTions
onE
suddenly Realized
that two notations on the saMe
      pIece of paper
automatically briNg
      About relationship
my Composing
is actuallY unnecessary

musIc
      Never stops it is we who turn away
again the worlD around
silEnce
sounds are only bubbles on iTs
surfacE
they buRst to disappear (thoreau)
when we Make
musIc
we merely make somethiNg
thAt
Can
more naturallY be heard than seen or touched

from ON ROBERT RAUSCHENBERG, ARTIST, AND HIS WORK

Conversation was difficult and correspondence virtually ceased. (Not because of the mails, which continued.) People spoke of messages, perhaps because they'd not heard from one another for a long time. Art flourished.

The goat. No weeds. Virtuosity with ease. Does his head have a bed in it? Beauty. His hands and his feet, fingers and toes long-jointed, are astonishing. They certify his work. And the signature is nowhere to be seen. The paintings were thrown into the river after the exhibition. What is the nature of Art when it reaches the sea?

Beauty is now underfoot wherever we take the trouble to look. (This is an American discovery.) Is when Rauschenberg looks an idea? Rather it is an entertainment in which to celebrate unfixity. Why did he make black paintings, then white ones (coming up out of the South), red, gold ones (the gold ones were Christmas presents), ones of many colors, ones with objects attached? Why did he make sculptures with rocks suspended? Talented?

I know he put the paint on the tires. And he unrolled the paper on the city street. But which of us drove the car?

from COMPOSITION AS PROCESS

NICHI NICHI KORE KO NICHI: EVERY DAY IS A BEAUTIFUL DAY
What if I ask thirty-two questions?
What if I stop asking now and then?
Will that make things clear?
Is communication something made clear?
What is communication?
Music, what does it communicate?
Is what's clear to me clear to you?
Is music just sounds?

Then what does it communicate?

Is a truck passing by music?

If I can see it, do I have to hear it too?

If I don't hear it, does it still communicate?

If while I see it I can't hear it, but hear something else, say an
    egg-beater, because I'm inside looking out, does the truck
    communicate or the egg-beater, which communicates?

Which is more musical, a truck passing by a factory or a truck
    passing by a music school?

Are the people inside the school musical and the ones outside
    unmusical?

What if the ones inside can't hear very well, would that change
    my question?

Do you know what I mean when I say inside the school?

Are sounds just sounds or are they Beethoven?

People aren't sounds, are they?

Is there such a thing as silence?

Even if I get away from people, do I still have to listen to
    something?

Say I'm off in the woods, do I have to listen to a stream babbling?

Is there always something to hear, never any peace and quiet?

If my head is full of harmony, melody, and rhythm, what happens
    to me when the telephone rings, to my peace and quiet, I
    mean?

And if it was European harmony, melody, and rhythm in my
    head, what has happened to the history of, say, Javanese
    music, with respect, that is to say, to my head?

Are we getting anywhere asking questions?

Where are we going?

Is this the twenty-eighth question?

Are there any important questions?

"How do you need to cautiously proceed in dualistic terms?"

Do I have two more questions?

And, now, do I have none?

Hilda Morley

NINE

I who stand at the edge of
the world & lean backward
to where my home was
once
    (at the edge of
    nothing no & the brink of
    all newness,
      & my clothes
    that were meant for another
    place,
      meant to be
    seen by a person no longer
    here, unseemly,
       as if
    smeared or crumpled
    or as if seams had opened,
    hems burst,
      unlikely
    rents appearing,
       everything
    fitting badly
Is this my body that was
loved by him—the same breasts small and
separate as they have always been,
     the same squareness
of shoulder,
   narrowness

of waist, round hips,
              hollows
of ribs showing
as always?
      Is this the head that was
caressed for roundness
                & fingers
that held it once now ashes
& the shape of nose once treasured,
                          eyes'
curving, all these coldly
now exposed to a hundred
winds from all the ends of
the universe
          Is it the same sun looks down on
my body walking with
its own particular movement & you
not there to see it?
An effigy dressed like a
scarecrow to frighten the birds away,
                        a walking
hollow with the name you once knew,
                          loved by
you—the skin & bones & flesh of
something called Hilda that you
once sensed & knew by a hundred
different names who
was spacious enough to give you
shelter & alive enough to
find her shelter in you,
              who are
now inside this little urn of ashes

THE EYE OPENED

for Bill de Kooning

Blue & yellow of the sun & green
streaks that slash, spatter
flame
      on flatness
            & 30 years ago
the reds & blacks, brown & greys
cutting & delving
          The movement
tossing more now,   but as
leaves branching,   less centrifugal—
a web in layers,
        and
still that hilarity
        that I
can't forget—word I used when
I first saw the *Women*
        & joy in
simultaneity,
      the contradictions
      (I know of them from
that man who was dearest
to me   who, in composing, thinking
loved "the other side of the coin")
as in the knowing

of what is & isn't   at
the same time,   in a single
moment:
      worlds leaning
against each other,
        turning
in & out of themselves,   there,

not there,   dropping, falling
away &
              rising up at once
                        as you said "But Nature
doesn't make me peaceful
                    It does the opposite"
(While my love made in his Duo for Oboe & Clarinet the sound of
insects humming in fury,
                    told his students,
pointing to the traffic on 14th Street: Compose
that!)
        And you out of
the clash of opposites—bay, roadway,
inlet,   green fields,   beach,
                            make not a
fusing or a blend   but an
enhancement:
                the earth's bowels
stirring,
            where the painting
paints you,   paints you in or
out   & the exchange is
mutual,   is process in
mutuality,
                to whatever extreme of furtherness
be opened,
                the colors stretching
as when an eye is opened   in meeting
with another eye,
                    the pupil & the iris
beneath the eyelid,
                    as voices
may overlap   & for a moment, can
seem the same,   spring out of
the one source,

                              walking on
Eighth Street & University Place,

                                        the eye opened making
essential fire.

FOR CREELEY

Whatever "wandering minstrel" look in
the spring of '54 (its wet beginning
in North Carolina)
                              & the hooded eye asking
really for nothing except to be
listened to
                    & then the extreme courtesy
                                        so little
seen in that particular place,
with the passion for Miles Davis—intensity
withheld—& gentleness of manner
almost insidious: those marked you
at that time, Creeley, in Black Mountain.
Somehow I associate them with
your hands & feet.
                              After
that time only bits of news, glimpses, and
your voice on the telephone saying
before anything else: "What can I
do for you?"—without hesitation,
startling me with its goodness,
                                        making
everything easy (no need to
ponder: how shall I say it?)
                              And always
your hands & feet like someone

mounting a wave
                    & descending
from it.

        What in you was cognizant
of the man I lived with,
the depth he embodied,
                  that surprising
kinship I rejoiced in,   wondering
how it was so, what side of you,
what aspect could reach toward him   & listening
inwardly, hear him,   watching,
see him,   his outreaching truth
                       I'm grateful that
you're there, winding,   unwinding
inside this coil of life,
                  grateful
that you can make me laugh when
I'm dismayed,   that your insights
delight me,   that you are able
to take in your stride whatever
befalls me,   even
the strangest,   most horrible.
                    I'm grateful
for the arc of you,
              all that has emerged out of
that first image:
        wandering minstrel.

"Asheville" by Willem de Kooning (1948)

The Phillips Collection

Edward Dorn

THE REVIVAL

Today I am a vast dirge.
Today I have not flown; like a great tired vulture
to pick off the dried crust
plastered around the body of Hope.
Today, picking small bits of shit is not my forte.

Yesterday, think of it! you were unspinning
tales of anti-cant, tales collected
five years ago. Who is not overwhelmed
by revival?

Today I am impatient with small horrors.
I scorn all but the millenial clan, the whales
will flush my own dismal phantoms like quails,
Today I am a vast dirge, my shoulders quake.

LITANY FOR A YELLOW LAMP

Outdoor lamps that light more
Than themselves are a burden
And destroy night where night
Is most local. Where night
Lays surely on pine needles
There is inevitable care.

Stop and go lights the importance
Of asphalt for those whose wild
Intentions are motor driven,
The intent is less endurable,
But there are left here and there those
Who can't categorize the moon,
Yellow, like some older street
Lamp, whose sanity brings no
Rape over sleeping leaves and
Whose light marks time, ambitious
Only in its own composition,
Awaiting its periodic heir.

THE 7TH

There was a time sitting in a room
I wanted to see everyone I ever knew
and of course I don't remember the bad ones
except a few. What a shock
to get over the embarrassment of using language.

That's why I write to you every day
I no longer have that tedious care.

STORE SCENE

Some woman stood there, in the aisle, waiting.
The child clutched roundly the coat, in handfuls,
The woman of whom I speak, sat, juxtaposed, on
The stair,

and felt the vibration, across,
of seeking fingers.

What made this not a linear event was
The difference of, a multiple humanity in,
The act, participating the way we independently
Were.
        I mean that the woman, that the child,
        are engaged with their intent.
        The stair held a point of wonder and
        I get my connection at the bottom

                step on which she, the woman
                of whom I speak, sat.

Most recent mother, the pangs still caught
In the breast, so lately assertive of more
Than motherhood, yet stiff with unweened attention.
When she spoke of the child, it was from the sloughed
Context, a woman that fell into tomorrow without
Taking off her clothes.

THE POET LECTURES FAMOUS POTATOES

He visited:
He said no, no emotion
said the poet
is not sentimental
(However didn't say what that means)
said he does not spill what he has
in him. He makes like a carpenter
makes his cabinet to hold things

objects, which were carved
and are placeable
                          and do not tip.

Uh be not so artlessly baleful
toward society. Be well dressed
but not too well dressed
(Of course everybody knows that)
Yes, he's just so,
neither a scholar nor not a scholar.

Schools he said, are those benches
of learning for the man of sensibility
or out to be, uh
he said something else
meaning—we're liberals, hyphen hip
the cats who argue all that business
they been talking about, but
let's hush it around, don't
praise Allen Ginsberg.

THE MOUNTAINS

for the painter, Raymond Obermayr

Like a distant rumble of undeclared war
the wind shakes all things on our ears
and it's like the water treatment
or a willful cat how the nerves
don't anymore fend for themselves.

The base of the mountains
are blue and flecks of moving brown
are there like a lingering image.

But above that base
comes the magenta higher mountains,
steps to green, a rise the eye
can only take, where again lingers yellow
and all runs to a high atmospheric orange
but cut
the deep black blue of
full day.

I know men men have perished here
there and all around.

Thus in a cut of all of it
there is the inferno we forget,
descends to the only red of fire.
To go down there is the whole
tension of its mystery.
All lingers. All passes in those hills.

One tempts the perfect
with suggested birds and men
suggested toil, one is reckless
enough to say they are there and forget.
And enough to leave all growth aside.
There is no frame for blue
but blue, but this is a late time
after blue was made.

And the earth herself
lets no such recessions loose.
You can move in the shadows, in that
wild blue, small towns
like specks flourish and go out
there is no coming back from the space
you make.

Paul Blackburn

7TH GAME: 1960 SERIES

—for Joel—

Nice day,
sweet October afternoon
Men walk the sun-shot avenues,

                    Second, Third, eyes
                    intent elsewhere
ears communing with transistors in shirt pockets
                Bars are full, quiet,
discussion during commercials
                  only
Pirates lead New York 4-1, top of the 6th, 2
Yankees on base,   1 man out

What a nice day for all this !
Handsome women, even
dreamy jailbait, walk
                nearly neglected :
men's eyes are blank
their thoughts are all in Pittsburgh

Last half of the 9th, the score tied 9-all,
Mazeroski leads off for the Pirates
The 2nd pitch he simply, sweetly
                CRACK!
belts it clean over the left-field wall

Blocks of afternoon
acres of afternoon

Pennsylvania Turnpikes of afternoon . One
                    diamond stretches out in the sun
                            the 3rd base line
                and what men come down
                it

        The final score, 10-9

Yanquis, come home

LOVE IN THE SOUTH   OR   THE MOVIES

Beauty is a promise of happiness
which is why we take pleasure in it
why we ache when we cannot possess it

What we have of it is on account
the ache
the pleasure

Once we possess it, it
comes as near to us as at noon
feeling the heat alone rising,
a man's shadow comes,

so close that we do not see it. What's

the good of a *mystique* like that?   Yet
' How miserable I am! ' and
' How beautiful the world is! '
are   2   cries
that arise from the same place

THE MARGIN

Late morning on this island: cocks
enchanted with the sun
compete across the mountains,
blossoms here already in February!

Excitedly, we sit here talking
nonsense in the sunlight.
The lemon tree is heavy,
these giddy roosters also crow at noon
just to hear each other.

A few good things are left on earth
and they are not manufactured.

Jonathan Williams

A VULNERARY

(for Robert Duncan)

one comes to language from afar, the ear
fears for its sound-barriers—

but one 'comes'; the language 'comes' for
The Beckoning Fair One

*plant you now, dig you
later,* the plaint stirs winter
earth . . .

air in a hornets' nest
over the water makes a
solid, six-sided music . . .

a few utterly quiet scenes, things
are very far away—*'form
is emptiness'*

comely, comely, love trembles
and the sweet-shrub

THE OLDEST & THE COOLEST

(for Archie Moore, on TV, post—Bobo Olson)

at 1:19
of the 3rd round—
the winner
and still
Champion
of the World!

busy, very busy, coming in:
"I set him up with a couple jabs and
he was right *there*; then
I hit him with a double righthand, I caught him with a left hook ...

whip/whap,
that's it!"

gloves cut off, ready to cut out, pocket
comb going *flip* 30 seconds later ...

"yes, man, a nice fighter; yes,
he shook me once; yes a left (note I was
moving by then, man);
yes, slow canvas, man; yes,
Rocky next... why'd I stare at him, man? why, man,

the eyes are
the mirrors of the soul, man"

Whether the Ancient One was entertaining us with Melville, Shakespeare,
Cervantes, or himself, we do not know...

ENTHUSIAST

literature—the way we ripen ourselves
by conversation, said
Edward Dahlberg . . .

we flower in talk, we slake
our thirsts in a brandy of heated speech, song
sweats through the pores,
trickles a swarm
into the sounding keyboard,

pollen falls
across the blackened paper . . .

always idle—before and
after
the act:

making meat
of vowels
in cells
with sticky feet

SYMPHONY NO. 5, IN C SHARP MINOR

> *"How blessed, how blessed a tailor to be! Oh that I had been born a commercial*
> *traveller and engaged as baritone at the Opera! Oh that I might give my*
> *Symphony its first performance fifty years after my death!"*
> —*Mahler, 1904*

I. FUNERAL MARCH

Mahler, from his studio on the 11th floor of the
Hotel Majestic, New York City, hears the cortege of a
fireman moving up Central Park West:

one roll of the drum

one road where the wind storms, where
Cherubim sing birds' songs
with human faces and hold the world
in human hands and drift on the gold road
where black wheels smash
all

one roll of the drum

II. STORMILY AGITATED

to be a block of flowers
in a wood

to be mindlessly in flower
past understanding

to be shone on
endlessly

to be *there*, there
and blessed

III. SCHERZO

one two three
one two three

little birds waltz to and fro
in the piano

at Maiernigg on the
Wörthersee

and up the tree:
cacophony

one two three

IV. ADAGIETTO

one feels
one clematis petal
fell

its circle
is all

glimmer on this pale
river

V. RONDO-FINALE

Schoenberg: "I should
even have liked to observe
how Mahler
knotted his tie,
and should have found that
more interesting and instructive
than learning how
one of our musical bigwigs composes
on a quote sacred subject
unquote

... An apostle
who does not glow
preaches heresy."

his tie was knotted
with éclat
on
the dead run!

Dan Rice and Robert Creeley at Black Mountain College (1955)

Photograph by Jonathan Williams

Joel Oppenheimer

THE DANCER
        for Katherine Litz

for Katy
        stands rooted, herself
to one spot
            becomes:
                        the only spot we know.

Grows, in this spot, among:
                        flowers
                        love
                        whatever's
her particular
            as we too
have particulars
            but she
flies free
        pulling.

Delight, unvarying
                        Katy dances;
her dance's conjure:
                        flowers;
her legs are suns to light
the seeds around, while
                        on the wooden floor
her feet
know mud, know snow, know
spring

AN ANSWER

what mercy is not
strained, what justice
not bought, what
love not used come thru.
my lady asks me
not without reason
where is pleasure in it. where sense.
my ear is not worth much
in these matters, tho it be
shelllike, and acute.
offer beyond dedication?
and a particular care.

THE LOVER

every time
the same way
wondering when
this when that.
if you were a
plum tree. if you
were a peach
tree.

N. B.

love is not memory, love
is the present act

is what have we done for
us lately, is where
am i, or you

you are sitting on a
rock in the moonlight
your red-blond hair
loose in the moonlight
you are crying

that was a long time
ago. a lot happened.

and if her hair sitting
before me is the same
shade, rarely found,

                    your hair
is not love, love is
the present act.

Larry Eigner

A FETE

The children were frightened by crescendoes
cars coming forward in the movies

That is, before they found out love,
that is, Comedy

                the cheeks blew
        music rises and continues

and the sea does

and there were no accidents today
the bombs showered us in the air

#292

in the air   the slant snow
     the bird rising away
  from the wild and bare tree

"THE WATER DRIPPING"

the water dripping
    seems to fit
  one pipe to another
       a secluded part of the world
     streams
       would fill over
        conduct down
      by vertical leaps
      to the horizontal
           or nearly that
      you see it
       interrupted by air
         the accurate
          slow
            as appears
             during the day
        there is no pulse
        for a clock
         in the rain
          irregular
              as it is too
        return of the same substance
        not quite perceived

"WHAT TIME IS"

What time is
    it day

    I may
  sleep

    hour on hour
or all the time, what
     a consideration, you
   pretty good,
what a question   forwards in
  a circle the
other way around it
    may
have gone, the thought
  of what to do   a tree
sits and birds come
   there's a word for each leaf, and each
        wall and
   a word for nothing

John Wieners

A POEM FOR RECORD PLAYERS

The scene changes

Five hours later and
I come into a room
where a clock ticks.
I find a pillow to
muffle the sounds I make.
I am engaged in taking away
from God his sound.

The pigeons somewhere
above me, the cough a
man makes down the hall,
the flap of wings
below me, the squeak
of sparrows in the alley.
The scratches I itch
on my scalp, a landing
of birds under the bay
window out my window.

                      Details
but which are here and
I hear and shall never
give up again, shall carry
with me over the streets
of this seacoast city,
forever,
      oh clack your
metal wings, god, you are

mine now in the morning.
I have you by the ears
in the exhaust pipes of a
thousand cars, gunning
their motors turning over
        all over town.

A POEM FOR MOVIE GOERS

I sit in the late evening
        in a quiet restaurant on
        the International Settlement of San Francisco.
My friends, the poets are gone.

Talk of opium and 4 days on horse
        riding across country. Talk of cancer
        sickness sweeping the world
As we, the poets sit. We who should be out
        on battlefields in silver suits
                drink our energies away. David
                talks of hanging wires with no connections.
        And I say we are the conductors.
No wonder Walt Whitman loved them

2

        The records change.
                Green vines hang
down one white column on the balustrade.
There is a marble terrace at my right
and my lover walks miles away.
                On the other side of town
                where the cable car goes down
                and the neon lights stay on all night.

Orange lamps along the wall
and oak leaves sprout too small
My lover's thoughts are not
                              of me at all.

CHARITY BALLS

I had a fellowship, but lived poorly
On slices of pizza.
Later, a career of washing lettuce;
but I have always been the same.
It's a question of acquiring a mastery of tone
Beneath the crystal chandaliers and champagne
on a glass table top.
At the age of five I thought Scarlett O'Hara
a fictional character. It was not until
The age of forty-eight I knew she was real.
Old clothes and bedroom slippers and a scarf
Wrapped around her head
In low cost tenement housing.
She began talking about my writing
And her sex life.
I'm curt by nature and dolorous.
But I knew if I worked hard I'd eventually make it.

Acknowledgments

Josef Albers, "Untitled," "It Was Not Meant to Be," and "More or Less" from *Poems and Drawings*, copyright © 2019 the Josef and Anni Albers Foundation.

Paul Blackburn, "7th Game: 1960 Series," "Love in the South or the Movies," and "The Margin" from *The Collected Poems of Paul Blackburn*, copyright © 1985 by Joan Blackburn.

John Cage, excerpts from "Composition as Process," "Forerunners of Modern Music," "On Robert Rauschenberg, Artist, and His Work," "Untitled," and "Indeterminacy" from *Silence: Lectures and Writings* © 1961 and excerpt from "Composition in Retrospect" in *X: Writings '79–'82* © 1983 by John Cage. Published by Wesleyan University Press and reprinted with permission.

Robert Creeley, "The Whip," "Two Ways of Looking in a Mirror," "The Picnic," "The Rhyme," "For W.C.W.," "Some Place," "The Rain," "Paul," and "To Think..." from *The Collected Poems of Robert Creeley, 1945-1975*, copyright © 2006 University of California Press. Used by permission.

Edward Dorn, "The Revival," "Litany for a Yellow Lamp," "The 7th," "Store Scene," "The Poet Lectures Famous Potatoes," and "The Mountains" from *Collected Poems*, copyright © 2012 the Estate of Edward Dorn. Used by permission of Carcanet Press Limited.

Robert Duncan, "Often I am Permitted to Return to a Meadow," "The Structure of Rime I," and "The Structure of Rime II" from *The Opening of the Field* © 1960; "Come, Let Me Free Myself," "Thank You For Love," and "Answering" from *Roots and Branches* © 1964; "Bring It Up from the Dark" from *Ground Work* © 2006 by Robert Duncan. Published by New Directions Publishing Corporation.

Larry Eigner, "A Fete," "#292," "The water dripping," and "What time is" from *The Collected Poems of Larry Eigner*, copyright © 2010 the Estate of Larry Eigner. Published by Stanford University Press.

R. Buckminster Fuller, "Untitled Epic Poem on the History of Industrialization" © 1962, 2019 and "No More Secondhand God" © 1963, 2019 the Estate of R. Buckminster Fuller.